Inventions That Shaped the World

THE
CALENDAR

P A T R I C I A   K .   K U M M E R

Franklin Watts
A Division of Scholastic Inc.
New York • Toronto • London • Auckland • Sydney
Mexico City • New Delhi • Hong Kong
Danbury, Connecticut

Photographs © 2005: akg-Images, London: 40 (Gilles Mermet), 18, 70, 71 (Musee Conde), 33, 39; Art Resource, NY: 65 (Alinari), 24 (Werner Forman), 22 (Erich Lessing), chapter openers, 19 top, 54 bottom (Reunion des Musees Nationaux), 31, 44 (Scala), 62 (Snark); Brown Brothers: 26, 70, 71; Bruce Coleman Inc./Derk R. Kuyper: 8; Corbis Images: 46 (Alinari Archives), cover bottom left, 7, 12, 28 (Bettmann), cover center, 60 (Gianni Dagli Orti), 16, 57, 68 (Royalty-Free), 20 (Adam Woolfit); Digital Vision: cover bottom right background; Getty Images/Photodisc Green: cover top left, cover top right; Hulton|Archive/Getty Images/MPI: 67; ImageState/SW Productions: 14; Mary Evans Picture Library: 37; Omni-Photo Communications/Popshots: 69; Peter Arnold Inc./Yasumaro Yaita/Astrofoto: 23 bottom; Photo Researchers, NY: 30 (Archive), chapter openers, 11 (Jean-Loup Charmet), 19 bottom (Rapho/DeSazo), 43 (John G. Ross), 9, 70, 71 (Eckhard Slawik); PhotoEdit/David Young-Wolff: 55; The Art Archive/Picture Desk: 23 top (Dagli Orti), 45 (Dagli Orti/Archbishops Palace Ravenna, Italy), 35 (Dagli Orti/Archivio di Stato di Siena), 54 top (Dagli Orti/Museo Correr, Venice), 66 (Eileen Tweedy/Sir John Soane's Museum); The Image Bank/Getty Images/Petrified Collection: cover bottom right; The Image Works/David Lassman/Syracuse Newspaper: 58; TRIP Photo Library/Helene Rogers: 5, 49, 52.

Cover design by Robert O'Brien
Book production by Tricia Griffiths Swatko

Library of Congress Cataloging-in-Publication Data

Kummer, Patricia K.
  The calendar / by Patricia K. Kummer.
    p. cm. — (Inventions that shaped the world)
  Includes bibliographical references and index.
  ISBN 0-531-12340-5 (lib. bdg.)   0-531-16720-8 (pbk.)
  I. Calendar—Juvenile literature. I. Title. II. Series.
   CE13.K86 2005
   529'.3—dc22   2004006914

CONTENTS

Chapter One   WHAT IS A CALENDAR?   5

Chapter Two   EARLY METHODS OF COUNTING DAYS, SEASONS, AND YEARS   17

Chapter Three   PEOPLE WHO HELPED CREATE THE MODERN CALENDAR   29

Chapter Four   DEVELOPMENT OF THE MODERN CALENDAR   37

Chapter Five   THE IMPORTANCE OF THE CALENDAR   51

Chapter Six   THE CALENDAR'S CONTINUING DEVELOPMENT   59

TIMELINE   70

GLOSSARY   72

TO FIND OUT MORE   74

INDEX   77

ABOUT THE AUTHOR   80

CHAPTER ONE

WHAT IS A CALENDAR?

Carvings on animal bones, arrangements of huge stones, marks on clay tablets, square boxes on sheets of paper, even recording the flooding of rivers. These methods are a few of the ways people have kept track of the passage of days, months, and years. From the beginning of human history, people have observed the passing of time. First they noticed a

The Aztec calendar was carved into a huge stone (above) with their sun god at its center. This ancient calendar had a 365-day year.

regular pattern of daylight and darkness, which came to be called a *day*. Next, they saw that about every twenty-nine or thirty days the moon went through the same phases, or cycle of changing shapes. People also noted that the sun's position in the sky changed during a cycle of approximately 365 days. Throughout thousands of years, they gradually used their measurements taken from observations of the sky to predict and record the timing of events on earth.

Definition of the Calendar

Because even the earliest people needed order in their lives, they organized time and placed it in sequence. This sequence of time is organized on what people around the world call a *calendar*. The calendar is a way of arranging the days of the year into *months* and *weeks*. Because each year has its own number, calendar time also allows people to keep track of past years and the events that occurred in them.

Because calendar time is *sequential*, each day is different. It happens once—never to be repeated. For example, January 26, 2004, occurred only once. When that day was over, it passed into history. To mark the passing of time, some people draw Xs through the days on the calendar. When one month ends, they turn over the page to a new calendar month. At the end of the year on December 31, they hang up or set out calendars for the new year.

Medieval astronomers made astronomical observations and took measurements to help them know when events would happen on earth.

Units of Time of the Calendar

The calendar organizes a year by dividing it into days, weeks, and months. The smallest unit on a calendar is the day. Simply stated, a day is the length of time it takes the earth to rotate on its axis. When one side of the earth faces the sun, there is daylight on that side of the earth. When one side of the earth is turned away from the sun, there is darkness or night on that side. A day can be measured from one midnight to the next, from one sunrise to the next, or from one sunset to the next. In most parts of the world, the day begins at midnight, or 12 A.M.

A larger unit of calendar time is the month. The word *month* comes from the Latin and Greek words for "moon." In many early calendars, the length of a month was based on the natural cycle of the **phases of the moon**. A lunar

This year-at-a-glance calendar shows sequential time for the course of a year.

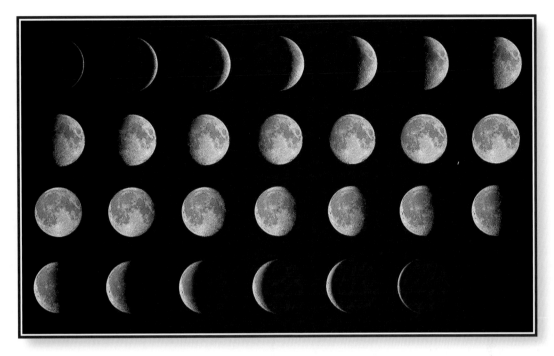

This image shows the moon in various phases of its cycle.

month is the length of time from one new moon to the next new moon. This is about 29.5 days. A lunar year of twelve months has 354 days. However, the modern calendar used throughout most of the world is based on the solar year of 365 days.

Throughout thousands of years, astronomers have tried to figure out the accurate length of the solar year. Today, people agree that the **year** is about 365 days long. That is about the amount of time required for the earth to make one complete revolution around the sun. Actually, the year is 365.24219 days long. This is called the tropical year. The modern calendar is based on the tropical year.

THE WEEK

The length of the day, the month, and the year is based on natural cycles of the earth, the moon, and the sun. Some historians believe that the seven-day week was based on the approximately seven days between each of the phases of the moon—new moon, first quarter, full moon, and last quarter. On the modern calendar, there is no relation between the phases of the moon and the beginning or ending of weeks of the year. Today's seven-day week is based on human traditions. In various cultures the week has ranged from five days to ten days. By the 1200s B.C., the Hebrews had a seven-day week. It was based on the creation story: God created the world in six days and rested on the seventh day. About 700 B.C., the Babylonians also had a seven-day week. They named the days of the week after the moon and the five planets that they had identified—Mars, Mercury, Jupiter, Venus, and Saturn. The Romans had an eight-day week. It was based on the length of time between market days.

Three Kinds of Calendars

There are three kinds of calendars: lunar, solar, and lunisolar. *Lunar calendars* are based on the cycles of the moon. They have a twelve-month year of about 354 days. Lunar calendars are not based on the earth's movement around the sun. As a result, the lunar year moves backward through the seasons. The Islamic calendar used today is an example of a lunar calendar.

This seventeenth-century French lunar calendar calculates the phases of the moon on any given date.

Solar calendars are based on the length of time it takes the earth to make one revolution around the sun. These calendars have a twelve-month year of 365 days. To keep in agreement with the seasons, an extra day is added in most years whose number can be divided by four. Those years are called *leap years*. The modern calendar that is used by most people throughout the world is a solar calendar.

This engraving of a diagram of the universe depicts the earth revolving around the sun, upon which solar calendars are based.

Lunisolar calendars combine elements of lunar and solar calendars. Lunisolar calendars are based on the cycles of the moon. However, lunisolar calendars add a month every two or three years. In that way, they stay in tune with the seasons of the solar calendar. The Hebrew calendar and the Chinese cultural calendar are examples of lunisolar calendars.

Inventions and the Calendar

It's not surprising that people have been working on finding better ways to measure, record, and organize time almost from the beginning of human life. The invention and development of the modern calendar seems like one of those things—like the wheel, writing, and currency—that just had to happen for people and civilization to progress. Without the calendar, how would businesses schedule meetings? How would governments know when to hold elections? How could families plan vacations? How would religions know when to celebrate holy days?

An invention usually develops from a need or a desire to do something more easily or to make life better. Someone with imagination (an inventor) begins to think about making a product or developing a process (an invention). Work on an invention can take years—even centuries (hundreds of years) or millennia (thousands of years). Sometimes inventions occur when two or more people work together, such as when the Wright brothers invented the airplane. Other

With so many people leading busy lives, the calendar allows families to organize their time in an orderly way.

inventions, such as currency, have developed in separate parts of the world at about the same time or at different times. This has happened because people in various parts of the world experienced the same needs. In the years before speedy transportation and instant communication, similar inventions or steps in an invention have occurred independently in different places. All of these circumstances are true of the development of the calendar.

Inventions also can develop as a result of earlier inventions or processes of doing something. For example, in the United States in the early 1800s, Eli Whitney used the idea of interchangeable parts to develop the process of mass production. In this way, he was able to fill an order of ten thousand muskets for the U.S. government in two years. About one hundred years later, Henry Ford invented the assembly line to mass-produce the Ford Model T. These automobiles were made with interchangeable parts. Although the modern calendar is not a mechanical invention such as the airplane, the assembly line, and the automobile, its development relied on earlier advances in scientific and mathematical knowledge.

If an invention is truly useful, as the automobile and the airplane proved to be, it becomes an important part of daily life. When this happens, improvements are made to the product. What has been true of the development of the automobile and other mechanical inventions is also true of the calendar. For example, the modern calendar is more accurate than the one it replaced. In addition, the physical form of the calendar has changed. Besides paper calendars, people use calendars on computers and on cellular phones.

Today, almost every person on earth uses the calendar in some way each day. A child in Germany might look at a calendar to see when the next school holiday occurs. An adult in Japan might write an appointment with a doctor in one of the calendar's squares. Before planning a business trip, a manager in the United States would check the calendar to be sure there wasn't a conflict with an already scheduled meeting or with a child's band concert.

The amazing thing is that all these people throughout the world use the same calendar—even though they live in different countries, speak different languages, and use different currencies. Since 1582, the modern calendar—also called the Gregorian, the Christian, or the Western calendar—has gradually been adopted as the official civil calendar by all countries. This has made it easier to travel and to conduct trade throughout the world. By using the same calendar, people around the world share something in common.

The day planner (above) helps people keep track of meetings, appointments, and special events in their lives.

EARLY METHODS OF COUNTING DAYS, SEASONS, AND YEARS

For thousands of years, the calendar has been the major tool people have used to organize their lives. The calendar was developed long before the clock or other instruments that measure minutes and hours. Early people didn't need to know what time it was. They didn't have trains to catch or time clocks to punch. They did need to know what month or season of the year it was—and what month or season was coming up. They needed this information to tell whether to move north or south to follow the movement of the herds of animals they hunted. Later, as people settled in villages and farmed land, they needed to know when to prepare the land for crops, when to plant seeds, and when to complete the harvest. These early people also scheduled special days to honor their gods. By observing the phases of the moon, the

This illumination from the 1400s depicts twelve farm tasks throughout a twelve-month calendar year.

location of the sun, and the changing seasons, early people developed calendars. These calendars helped them determine when to schedule the important events in their lives.

Prehistoric Calendars: Bones and Wall Paintings

Perhaps the earliest evidence of people keeping track of time is an animal's bone. One particular bone dates back to about 28,000 B.C. It was found near present-day Dordogne, France. On this bone, a prehistoric person had carved circles and crescents that represented the phases of the moon. Archaeologists have found similar carved bones in other parts of Europe and in Africa.

Other prehistoric people drew calendars, as well as animals, on cave walls. About 13,000 B.C., also in the Dordogne area of France, in what are now known as the Lascaux caves, these early people made several rows of dots. Archaeologists think that the dots represent the moon's twenty-nine-day cycle.

A reindeer antler from 28,000 B.C. found in Dordogne, France, was used as a lunar calendar.

In this Lascaux cave in Dordogne, France, prehistoric people drew a line of dots, as well as animals, on cave walls. The dots are believed to stand for the moon's cycle.

Why did these people track the cycles of the moon? And what's more, why did they record the cycles? By knowing which nights would have moonlight, they could plan various events. Perhaps they hunted animals that were out and about at night. Maybe they held ceremonies for their gods. To create truly useful calendars, people had to keep track of the moon's phases for a full cycle of the seasons. Then, they could prepare for the future. For example, by knowing the number of new moons between the warmest days of summer and the first frost, they could complete their hunts and have enough food for the coming winter.

STONEHENGE: AN EARLY LUNISOLAR CALENDAR

Between about 3100 B.C. and 1500 B.C., prehistoric people in Britain built Stonehenge on Salisbury Plain. Astronomers today are sure that this circular structure was used as a calendar. Holes dug around the circle's outer edge seem to mark a lunar month. About 180 huge stones were erected in a pattern within the circle. Toward the center of the circle is the flat Altar Stone. Outside the circle, a shorter stone, called the Heel Stone, was erected. The Heel Stone is in line with the Altar Stone. On the summer solstice (June 21) and the winter solstice (December 21), a person standing at the Altar Stone can see the sun rise over the Heel Stone.

Early Written Lunar Calendars

From Mesopotamia to China to Greece, the world's first written calendars were based on the twelve-month lunar year. Mesopotamian people living in what is now southern Iraq are credited with writing down the first lunar calendar, sometime around 2600 B.C. This calendar had alternating months of twenty-nine and thirty days for a 354-day year. The Mesopotamian calendars were written on clay tablets using symbols called cuneiforms. About 2357 B.C. the Chinese developed a similar calendar. About 2100 B.C. the Mesopotamians devised a calendar year of 360 days. That brought their calendar more in line with the seasons— the solar year. But it was still not quite right. When the calendar became too far out of sync with the seasons, the king would have extra months added to the year.

In the 700s B.C., a Mesopotamian king ordered that five extra days be added to the end of the year. Eventually, the Mesopotamians devised a calendar that was on a nineteen-year cycle. Every two or three years during that cycle a thirteenth month was added. With these changes, the Mesopotamians were using a lunisolar calendar. Between 770 B.C. and 476 B.C., the Chinese also arrived at this nineteen-year cycle.

The ideas of the Mesopotamian calendar spread through-out the ancient Middle East and Mediterranean worlds. In 587 B.C., a Mesopotamian people known as the Babylonians

This clay tablet was used as an astrological calendar by the ancient Mesopotamians.

conquered Jerusalem and held the Hebrew people captive until about 520 B.C. While in Babylon, the Hebrews adopted the Mesopotamian nineteen-year cycle, which is similar to the present-day Hebrew calendar.

Early Solar Calendars

The Egyptians also started out with a lunar calendar. In fact, they are believed to have started using it in 4241 B.C., about 1,600 years before the Mesopotamians started writing down their calendar. The Egyptian calendar was arranged into three seasons of four months each. Winter was the growing season; spring was for harvesting; summer saw the Nile River flood. This flood brought rich soil to the Egyptian fields. Their calendar, however, did not help them predict the annual flooding of the Nile River.

Then, the Egyptians noticed something in the sky: Sirius, the Dog Star, in the constellation Canis Major. Sirius was the brightest star in the sky. It appeared just before sunrise shortly before the Nile flooded. For three years, this happened every 365 days. From this knowledge, the Egyptians made a calendar year of twelve thirty-day months with five days at the end. Then, they could tell when to complete their harvest and move out of the river

Egyptian calendars were designed around the seasons. This illustration depicts the spring harvest.

Sirius is the brightest star to shine in the night sky. The ancient Egyptians used it to develop their calendar.

valley ahead of the flood. Every fourth year, however, Sirius's appearance and the flooding happened one day later. Astronomers and farmers wanted an extra day added to the calendar every four years to make it accurate. Priests would not allow it, though. They thought the calendar was too sacred to change. So the Egyptian calendar remained inaccurate.

THE DOG DAYS OF AUGUST

Today, people sometimes refer to the "dog days of August" as a hot, slow, still time. The phrase comes from the prominence of Sirius, the Dog Star, during the summer month of August.

On the other side of the world, in what is now the Yucatán in Mexico, Belize, and Guatemala, the Maya also had developed a calendar based on the sun. By 1000 B.C., they were using a 365-day calendar divided into eighteen months of twenty days each, plus five extra days.

This Mayan relief depicts a single date in the calendar. Each date had both the name of an animal and a number.

The Early Roman Calendar

According to legend, Rome's first calendar was introduced in 753 B.C.—the same year that the city of Rome was founded. This calendar had ten months with a year of only 304 days. The months were named Martius (Mars), Aprilis ("Blooming Time"), Maius (a Roman goddess), Junius (Juno, queen of the gods), Quintilis, Sextilis, September, October, November, and December. The last six names stood for the numbers five through ten.

In 700 B.C., a Roman emperor added two months—Januarius and Februarius—to the end of the year. That gave the Roman year 355 days. It was one day longer than the lunar year because the Romans believed even numbers were unlucky. Every two years, the priests were to add twenty-two or twenty-three days during February. This made the average Roman year 366 to 366.5 days long. Thus, the Roman calendar was also lunisolar. As with all other lunisolar calendars, the Roman calendar had problems. The year ran slower than the seasons, or solar year. In addition, the priests sometimes played with the length of the year. They would add or take away days to lengthen or shorten terms of office for government leaders.

The early Roman calendar also had a strange way of numbering the days of the month. *Kalends* was the first day of the month, which was also the day after a new moon. The English word "calendar" comes from *kalends*. *Nones* marked the beginning of the first quarter of the moon, which was on the fifth or seventh day of the month. *Ides* marked the full moon, which was the thirteenth or fifteenth day of the month. All other days were numbered backward from the three named days. So if March 15 was the Ides of March, March 12 was known as four days before the Ides of March.

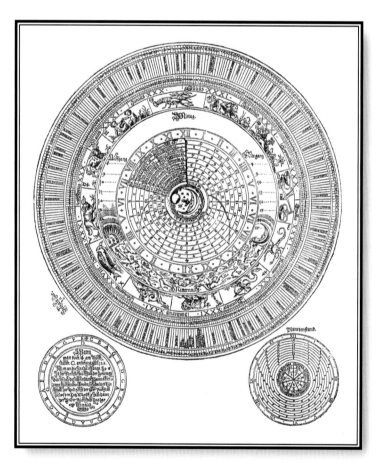

This Roman calendar shows all twelve months. The outer edge shows the eight days of the Roman week, which were the letters A through H.

RED-LETTER DAYS

People sometimes say, "Well, this was certainly a red-letter day." They mean the day was important for some reason. Perhaps they got a new job or a raise. Maybe an athlete set a world record. The expression "red-letter day" comes from the Roman calendar. Each day in the Roman week was given a letter from *A* through *H*. These letters ran down the left side of a Roman calendar. Most of the letters on the calendar were written in black paint or ink. The letters for holidays or special events, however, were in red. This tradition continues on modern calendars. On church calendars, for example, the numbers for Sundays and holy days are usually in red.

The astronomers and calendar makers in these ancient civilizations could not design a calendar that would remain consistent, accurate, and in tune with the seasons. When they tried to line up the lunar and solar years, they would have to add an extra month every few years. Sometimes the priests or kings would forget or would add too many. In addition, these ancient calendars were difficult to understand, especially for the majority of people who could not read. Also, each calendar year did not have its own number. Years were counted by a king's reign or from the founding of a dynasty or a city. For example, in Babylonia the year 596 B.C. would have been written as "The Tenth Year of the Reign of King Nebuchadnezzar II." These problems were solved with the development of the modern calendar.

Omar Khayyam, a great Persian mathematician and astronomer, worked on calculating the Persian calendar.

CHAPTER THREE

PEOPLE WHO HELPED CREATE THE MODERN CALENDAR

Several people played important roles in the development of the modern calendar. Most of them were political or religious leaders with power and influence over large numbers of people across vast areas of land. These leaders took the advice of scientists. They also called councils and set up commissions to determine an accurate calendar year. Only powerful persons could order reforms for the calendar's accuracy and enforce the use of a single calendar.

Julius Caesar

During the last years of the Roman Republic, Julius Caesar (about 100–44 B.C.) rose to power. Under his leadership as general, Roman troops conquered the land known as Gaul (58–50 B.C.). Today, this area includes France, Belgium, the

Netherlands, and part of Germany. Following these victories, the Roman Senate ordered Caesar to give up his armies. Instead, he crossed the Rubicon River into Rome with his troops and started a civil war in 49 B.C. His main opponent in the civil war was Roman general Pompey. Caesar followed Pompey to Egypt, where Pompey was killed. While Caesar was in Egypt, he met the astronomer Sosigenes and learned that Egypt's calendar was based on the sun.

Roman leader Julius Caesar ordered reforms to the Roman calendar, which resulted in the Julian calendar.

When Caesar returned to Rome in 46 B.C., the Senate appointed him dictator. With such great power, Caesar made many political and economic reforms within a few months. He limited the terms of office of many elected officials, put his own people in important offices, and took away some of the Senate's power. Caesar forgave many of the debts owed by Romans. His most important and long-lasting reform, however, was the calendar.

Some Roman calendars were carved in marble, some others stone. They were hung in public buildings.

Besides being dictator, Caesar was also the *pontifex maximus*, or high priest. The high priest was in charge of keeping the calendar accurate. Caesar, however, was busy with other things. By 46 B.C., the Roman calendar was running ahead of the solar year by at least two months. To remedy the situation, Caesar called scientists and mathematicians, including Sosigenes, to Rome. By January 1, 45 B.C., Rome had a new calendar based on the solar year of 365.25 days. Every fourth year, now known as leap year, was to have one additional day. This reformed calendar became known as the Julian calendar. It formed the basis for the modern calendar used throughout the world today.

BEWARE THE IDES OF MARCH

Julius Caesar did not live to complete his reforms or to enjoy the new calendar. On March 15, 44 B.C., he was assassinated by a group of senators. Caesar had been warned by a fortune-teller to "beware the Ides of March." The Ides of March was the fifteenth of that month. Even with Caesar's new calendar, the days were still counted based on the Kalends, Nones, and Ides.

Pope Gregory XIII and the Commission to Reform the Calendar

More than 1,600 years after Caesar's death, calendar reform again took place in Rome. On May 14, 1572, Ugo Buoncompagni (1502–1585) was elected pope of the Roman Catholic Church. He took the name Gregory XIII. The modern calendar is called the Gregorian calendar because Gregory XIII's work led to the reform of the Julian calendar.

Before becoming pope, Buoncompagni had attended the Council of Trent (1545–1563). This church council worked to reform abuses in the Catholic Church. By

GREGORIVS·XIII·PON·MAX

Pope Gregory XIII reformed the Julian calendar to what is now known as the Gregorian calendar, the one that is followed today.

making reforms, the Catholic Church hoped to regain many of the people who had broken away and joined the new Protestant churches.

When Buoncompagni became pope, he appointed committees to enact the council's reforms, which included reforming the calendar. By this time, the Julian calendar year was ten days ahead of the seasonal year. The first day of spring, which was supposed to fall about March 21, occurred on March 11. Because the dating of Easter was based on the March 21 date, this meant that Easter was not being celebrated on the correct date.

In 1572, Gregory XIII established a commission of ten men to reform the calendar. The work of two of those men—Aloysius Lilius and Christopher Clavius—formed the basis of the new calendar. Lilius (1510–1576), a doctor and astronomer from southern Italy, solved the problem of designing an accurate calendar. Just before he died in 1576, Lilius completed the book that set forth his ideas for calendar reform. Lilius's brother Antonio Lilius presented the book to Gregory XIII and took his brother's place on the commission. In the book, Lilius stated how to determine the length of the year, what the standard length of the year should be, how to be more accurate with leap years, and how to make up for the ten days by which the calendar had fallen behind. These matters will be explained in chapter four.

The pope gave Lilius's book to Christopher Clavius (1537–1612). He was a Jesuit priest from Bavaria, which is now part of Germany. Clavius was also a famous mathematician and astromomer. He read Lilius's book and agreed with his thoughts. Clavius presented Lilius's ideas for calendar reform to the commission, explained them, and got them passed. In March 1582, the pope issued an order that the commission's calender would go into

Christopher Clavius points out how to reform the Julian calendar, as Pope Gregory XIII and the reform commission look on.

effect on October 15, 1582. This new calendar became known as the Gregorian calendar. Gregory died three years later at the age of eighty-three. Clavius spent the rest of his life promoting the new calendar. He even wrote an eight-hundred-page book on how dates should be calculated through A.D. 5000.

THE FIRST CONTRACT TO PUBLISH GREGORIAN CALENDARS

Pope Gregory XIII wanted to reward the Lilius family for Aloysius's work on calendar reform. In 1583, Gregory awarded Antonio Lilius, Aloysius's brother, exclusive rights to publish the new calendar for ten years. But the demand for the calendars was so great that Antonio could not print them fast enough. As a result, the pope withdrew the contract.

CHAPTER FOUR

DEVELOPMENT OF THE MODERN CALENDAR

The early calendars of the Mesopotamians, the Egyptians, and the Romans had several drawbacks. They quickly became inaccurate, were hard to set up, and were difficult to read. An improved calendar was needed. First, the new calendar had to be accurate. It had to stay in line with the seasons. Most of the early calendars ran fast and got ahead of the seasons, although the Roman calendar lagged behind the seasons. Second, a

In Rome, calendars were found on walls for the public to read.

37

reformed calendar had to be easy to create and maintain. In other words, it shouldn't have to be tinkered with every few years by adding extra months. Third, the calendar had to be easy for people to understand and read. Fourth, the calendar had to be accepted over a large part of the world. In that way, traders, travelers, and diplomats would not have to convert dates from their calendar to that of the country they were visiting. Fifth, the calendar should be a way to mark and record consecutive years. Every year should have its own number, such as 1215, 1582, or 2005.

Unlike many other inventions, the calendar was not developed in a laboratory or a workshop. Instead, the major development of the modern calendar took place in the palaces of Julius Caesar and Pope Gregory XIII. Wires, nuts, and bolts did not build the calendar. The calendar received its frame and structure from mathematical formulas based on astronomical observations and measurements.

The First Stage of Calendar Reform: The Julian Calendar

By 46 B.C., the Roman lunar calendar was totally out of line with the seasons. The calendar showed September, a month in the fall, when it was really early summer. Julius Caesar decided to reform and simplify the calendar. He wanted a calendar that was accurate and could easily be used in all the lands under Rome's control. These lands

The development of the calendar was based upon astronomical observations and mathematical formulas.

reached to what are today northern Europe, northern Africa, and much of the Middle East.

Sosigenes was a Greek astronomer who lived in Roman-controlled Egypt. Caesar called Sosigenes to Rome to help with calendar reform. Sosigenes recommended that Caesar replace the Roman calendar with a solar calendar similar to Egypt's. A solar calendar would eliminate the need to add a month every few years. Rome's solar calendar would have

The early Roman calendar was not in line with the seasons. This third-century Roman floor mosaic depicts the month of September.

twelve months totaling 365.25 days. Each month would have thirty or thirty-one days, except February, which would usually have twenty-eight days. To make up the one-quarter of a day, February would have twenty-nine days every four years.

A RHYME FOR THE DAYS IN THE MONTH

For hundreds of years people have had trouble remembering how many days are in each month. In 1555, an English poet wrote a rhyme to help people with that problem. A version of that rhyme is still used today:

Thirty days has September,
April, June, and November.
February has twenty-eight alone,
All the rest have thirty-one.
Excepting leap-year—that's the time
When February's days are twenty-nine.

In the new calendar, Caesar kept the method for numbering the days of the month from the old Roman calendar. However, Kalends, Nones, and Ides were no longer tied to phases of the moon. But Caesar kept the same dates for public holidays and for religious festivals to honor the gods. Also, the months were still not divided into weeks.

"THE YEAR OF CONFUSION"

To put Rome's new calendar in line with the seasons, Sosigenes added ninety days—about three months—to the Roman year of 355 days. That gave the year 46 B.C. a total of 445 days. Because of the extra days, the year 46 B.C. was called the Year of Confusion. Officials didn't know if they should collect taxes for the extra months. Businesspeople weren't sure how to figure interest on loans. Taxes and interest were figured on a yearly basis but paid on a monthly basis.

On January 1, 45 B.C., the new calendar, now known as the Julian calendar, went into effect. Rome had what was at the time the world's most accurate calendar. There were still problems, however. The year of 365.25 days is eleven minutes and fourteen seconds longer than the true solar, or tropical, year. This meant that every 128 years the Julian calendar would have "gained" a day and be running another day earlier than the seasons. Astronomers in Caesar's time knew this but did not have the mathematical knowledge to correct the error. Their use of Roman numerals made multiplication and division difficult. Although they used fractions, the much more precise decimal had not yet been invented.

By 8 B.C., minor changes had been made to the Julian calendar. First, in 44 B.C., the Roman Senate changed the name of the seventh month, Quintilis, to Julius (July), in honor of Julius Caesar. He had been born in that month. Then in 8 B.C., the Senate honored Augustus Caesar, Rome's first emperor (27 B.C.–A.D. 14) by naming a month for him. They changed the name of the eighth month, Sextilis, to Augustus (August). Augustus had won many victories in Sextilis, and one of his names was Octavian, which means "eight."

Changes Continue Under the Christian Church

The calendar played an important role in the early Christian church. Christianity had spread throughout the Roman Empire. In the early A.D. 300s, the Roman emperor

Constantine had become a Christian. In 325, he called the Christian bishops to the Council of Nicaea. They were to set down the basic beliefs of the Christian church. In addition, they were to decide on an accurate method for determining Easter. Easter is the Christian holy day that celebrates the resurrection of Jesus Christ three days after his death on the cross. That event had occurred in the early spring sometime after March 21 in A.D. 30. The bishops determined that

The month of August is named after Roman Emperor Augustus Caesar.

Easter would be the first Sunday after the first full moon after March 21. The date for Easter is still determined in this way. Constantine also established a seven-day week for the empire, with Sunday as a day of rest.

In 525, Pope John I asked Christian monk and scholar Dionysius Exiguus (about 470–544) to draw up a table of Easter dates through the year A.D. 626. Dionysius did that and also changed the way that years were numbered. At that time, the B.C.–A.D. dating system had not been

43

The Council of Nicaea's bishops decided on a method to determine the dating of Easter.

invented. Years were numbered from the first year of the Emperor Diocletian's rule. Diocletian had persecuted Christians. For that reason, Dionysius decided to number the years starting with the year of Christ's birth. Dionysius called that year A.D. 1. *A.D.* stands for *Anno Domini,* "in the Year of the Lord." The years before Christ's birth were numbered backward from 1 *B.C.* However, Dionysius's calculations of Christ's birth were wrong. Christ was actually born no later than the year that is now called 4 B.C. It took several hundred years for the B.C.–A.D. dating system to become commonplace.

This marble tablet displays Easter dates for the years A.D. *532–566.*

ADVANCES IN MATH HELP THE CALENDAR

Before European people could devise an accurate calendar year, they had to adopt three advances in mathematics: Arabic numerals, zero as a number, and the decimal point. What people today call Arabic numerals were invented in India during the A.D. 200s. Through trade with India, Islamic Arabs adapted this number system during the A.D. 700s. Islamic Arabs also spread two other Indian math inventions: the use of zero as a number and the decimal point. By 1200, these three advances in math had reached Europe through contact with Arab traders. A few European scholars began using Arabic numerals, the

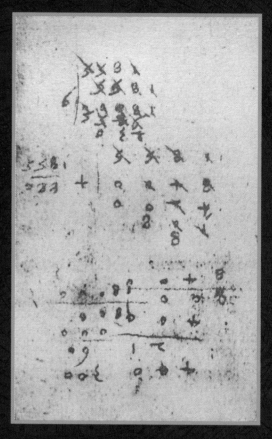

zero, and the decimal point, as shown in this illustration. With them, mathematicians could multiply and divide faster and more easily. Astronomers could also make more accurate calculations about the motion of the heavenly bodies. Thus, they could make a more accurate calendar year—one that was closer to the length of the tropical year of 365.24219 days.

The Second Stage of Calendar Reform: The Gregorian Calendar

From at least the A.D. 1200s, European scientists had been calling on popes to reform the Julian calendar. Because those scientists were using Arabic numerals, the zero, and decimals, they could determine a more accurate calendar year. The Julian calendar was by then several days ahead of the solar year and the seasons. All of western Europe was united through the Roman Catholic Church. Christians in Russia and what is now Greece and other countries to the east were in the Eastern Orthodox Church. As the head of the Roman Catholic Church, only the pope could issue a reform that would affect the entire western world. Finally in the 1570s, Pope Gregory XIII set up the commission for calendar reform. By that time, the Julian calendar was ten days ahead of the solar year.

The commission decided to use a calculation as close to the true motion of the sun as possible for the length of the calendar year. (Remember, at that time scientists still thought that the sun revolved around the earth.) The length of the calendar year was determined to be 365 days, 5 hours, 49 minutes, and 12 seconds. This is only twenty-six seconds slower, or less, than the true solar year.

The commission then decided how to make up for the slightly less than one-quarter extra day each year. They kept the idea of a leap year every four years in years divisible by four. However, years ending in two zeroes that could not evenly be divided by four hundred (1700, 1800, and 1900) would no longer be leap years. That would prevent the calendar year from falling behind the true year by three days every four hundred years. By 4909, the Gregorian calendar will be only one day ahead of the true solar year.

Next, the commission decided how to make up for the ten days that the Julian calendar had gained through the years. It did this by making October 1582 ten days shorter. In 1582, October 4 was followed by October 15. This upset many people who thought they had lost ten days. They really hadn't—only the calendar had changed. However, the loss of the ten days did cause short-term problems. For example, when should birthdays, anniversaries, and saints' days that fell between October 5 and October 14 be celebrated that year?

The commission also created a new method to determine the accurate date of Easter. In both the Julian and Gregorian calendars, Easter is celebrated on the first Sunday after the first full moon after March 21. In the Gregorian reform, however, a complicated mathematical formula was invented for determining the date of that full moon.

Countries that were under the influence of the Roman Catholic Church quickly adopted the new calendar. Countries under the influence of other religions, however, stayed on the Julian calendar for some time. Gradually, though, almost all the countries in the world adopted the Gregorian calendar. It is now the world's official calendar. Even countries that have a religious calendar as their official calendar use the Gregorian calendar for business and world affairs. For example, Saudi Arabia uses the lunar Islamic calendar, and Israel uses the lunisolar Hebrew calendar, but they also use the Gregorian calendar.

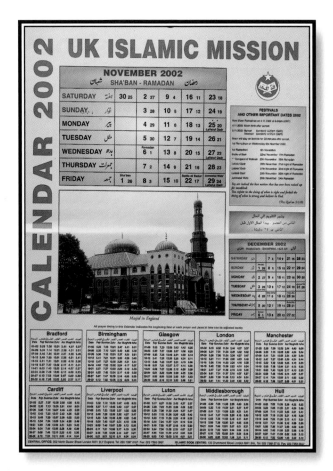

The Islamic calendar follows the cycles of the moon. It is based on the Qu'ran, Islam's holy book.

MAJOR COUNTRIES ADOPT
THE GREGORIAN CALENDAR

Country	Year Adopted	Days Lost*
Spain, Portugal, France, and their American colonies	1582	10
Austria	1583	10
Protestant states of Germany, Denmark	1700	10
Great Britain and its American colonies	1752	11
Sweden	1753	11
Japan	1873	
Egypt	1875	
China	1912	
Russia	1918	13
Greece	1924	13
Turkey	1926	

*This number applies only to countries that changed from the Julian calendar. The other countries had never used the Julian calendar.

CHAPTER FIVE

THE IMPORTANCE OF THE CALENDAR

Most of the calendars discussed so far, including the Julian and Gregorian calendars, are civil calendars. They are meant to be used by countries and their people to keep track of various matters. That is why leaders of countries had to approve the adoption of the Gregorian calendar. Although the modern or Gregorian calendar is recognized by all countries, other calendar years are still used for religious or cultural purposes.

Religious and Cultural Calendars

Two examples of calendars not connected to the Gregorian calendar are the Hebrew and Islamic religious calendars. The Chinese calendar is also not tied to the Gregorian. It's a cultural calendar that is based on tradition rather than on any religion. All of these calendars started in a different year. What's more, the first day of each of these calendar years falls in a different month than the first day of the Gregorian calendar year.

In addition, the Julian calendar is still the official calendar of the Eastern Orthodox Church. The Greek, Russian, and Ukrainian churches are the major Orthodox churches. All over the world, people who belong to these churches follow the Julian calendar for Christian religious holidays. That means Orthodox Christians usually celebrate Easter and Christmas after Christians who use the Gregorian calendar. Orthodox Christians use the Gregorian calendar for all nonreligious matters.

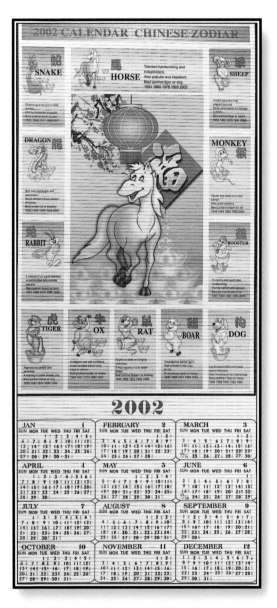

The Chinese lunar calendar names each year after an animal. The Chinese believe that the animal ruling the year in which they were born has a great influence on their personality.

MAJOR CALENDARS IN USE TODAY

Calendar	Year Number in 2005	Based On	Starts on This Date in the Gregorian Calendar
Gregorian	2005	Birth of Christ	January 1, 2005
Julian	2005	Birth of Christ	January 14, 2005
Islamic	1426	Flight of Muhammad	February 10, 2005
Chinese	4703	Legend	February 9, 2005
Hebrew	5766	Estimated year of creation	October 4, 2005

The Calendar and Economic Life

At first, the development of the Julian and Gregorian calendars affected mainly people in cities. Merchants, craftsmen, and traders used the calendar to accurately schedule the production, shipment, and delivery of goods. Bankers and their clients could figure the number of days that interest should be charged for loans and on what day of each month payments on the loans should be made.

Throughout many centuries, businesses have divided the year into four quarters that ended on the last days of March, June, September, and December. They figured their profits and losses on a quarterly basis. Today businesses operate on what is called the *fiscal year*. For some, the fiscal year begins on January 1 and ends on December 31. For others, the fiscal year begins on July 1 and ends on June 30.

53

The calendar was quite helpful to merchants who relied on it for keeping track of deliveries and shipments of goods.

PAUPER'S CALENDARS

Most of the Julian and Gregorian calendars were produced for people who could read. By the 1300s, calendars were also made for those unable to read. They were called pauper's calendars. Pictures and diagrams gave information about religious feasts. Drawings also provided advice about when to perform farm tasks.

The Calendar Industry

In the centuries since Gregory XIII gave Antonio Lilius a contract to produce calendars, the calendar industry has become a big business. The production and sale of calendars is a $5 billion industry in the United States alone. Today, 98 percent of homes in the United States have at least one calendar. Businesses, schools, governments, and other organizations also use calendars every day.

About 500 million calendars are printed and published every year in the United States. That includes wall calendars, foldout and stand-up calendars, desktop planning calendars, calendars on mouse pads and on refrigerator magnets, and CD-ROM calendars. Not included in the 500 million calendars are the many laminated yearly calendars about the size of a business card that people carry in their wallets.

The sale of calendars is a big business in the United States.

People and the Calendar

As has been discussed, religion and the history of the calendar were closely linked. Since the beginning of Christianity, the Julian calendar and the early Gregorian calendar regulated people's lives by telling them of holy days, saints' days, and periods of fasts and feasts. Between going to church and going to work, most people didn't have time to schedule much else. Throughout the centuries, however, the church lost most of its control over people's daily lives. In fact, some historians and archaeologists have even stopped using A.D. and B.C. to number years. Instead, they use CE (Common Era) and BCE (Before the Common Era). They don't think it is appropriate for people of other religions to have to use terms referring to Christ.

For most people, the calendar is a useful tool. Some people, however, seem to let the calendar rule their lives. They often overload their schedules and become stressed trying to get everything done. Today, the calendar helps people keep track of public holidays such as Presidents' Day and Labor Day, school holidays, and sporting events. Perhaps the most important days that people mark on their calendars are birthdays and anniversaries. They don't want to forget these dates.

Important reminders fill up this calendar.

LEAP-YEAR BIRTHDAYS

When do people born on Leap Day, February 29, celebrate their birthdays in *common years*? A common year is any year that is not a leap year. People born on February 29 usually have their birthday parties on February 28. Why would they want to wait until March 1? Leap-day babies have their own club. It's the World Wide Leap Year Birthday Club, with more than four hundred members. Each leap day they can meet in Anthony, a town on the Texas/New Mexico border. The town is known as the Leap Year Capital of the World. The World Wide Leap Year Festival is held there every four years.

The date that caused the most excitement in recent years was January 1, 2000. On that date, the world celebrated the beginning of the third millennium—two thousand years—since the birth of Christ. Many calendar perfectionists had two problems with this celebration. First of all, historians have proved that according to the A.D./B.C. counting system, Christ was really born no later than 4 B.C. Second, because there was no year zero, the third millennium didn't actually begin until January 1, 2001. Nevertheless, many people watched their televisions all day to see people in the rest of the world ring in the New Year of 2000.

New Year's Eve 1999 created much excitement for people who looked forward to entering a new millennium.

THE CALENDAR'S CONTINUING DEVELOPMENT

The Gregorian calendar is the world's most accurate calendar in use today. It's easy to set up and to read. The leap-year cycle has become automatic. Yet, since the late 1700s, various groups have called for further calendar reform. France even completely changed its calendar for several years. In addition, the format of the calendar continues to change.

The Calendar from the French Revolution: The Calendar of Reason

From September 22, 1792, to December 31, 1805, France went off the Gregorian calendar. During the French Revolution and First French Republic, France's leaders wanted the

During the French Revolution, France adopted its own calendar.

government to be completely separate from the Roman Catholic Church. That meant doing away with the calendar that had been reformed by a pope. France's new calendar was known as the Calendar of Reason. It had 365 days with a leap day every four years. Each month had only thirty days. To bring the year to 365 days, a five-day festival was added at the end of the year. Each month had three weeks. Each week was ten days long. The Calendar of Reason had its own numbering system for years. The year 1792 became the Year 1. That year marked the beginning of the French Republic.

The Calendar of Reason worked well within France, but it made conducting business with other countries difficult. In 1804, or Year 13, Napoleon Bonaparte had the pope crown him emperor of France. As of January 1, 1806, Napoleon put France back on the Gregorian calendar.

Perennial Versus Annual Calendars

The Gregorian calendar is an annual calendar because it is not exactly the same each year. The months do not start on the same day during the year or from year to year. Perennial calendars, however, look exactly the same each year. The months start on the same days within the year and from year to year. Since the 1800s, there have been proposals for a perennial calendar to replace the Gregorian.

In 1834, the International Fixed Calendar was first suggested. This calendar would have thirteen months of twenty-eight days for a total of 364 days. The 365th day would come after December 28. The extra day for leap year would be added after June 28. The thirteenth month would be added between June and July. It would be called Sol, meaning "Sun." The convenience of this calendar is that every month begins on a Sunday, ends on a Saturday, and has four equal weeks of seven days. This calendar, however, would cause problems for businesses that divide the year into four quarters of three months each. From time to time, various groups try to gain support for the International Fixed Calendar.

PERPETUAL CALENDAR

Perpetual means continuing on forever. The perpetual calendar is a chart for finding the day of the week for any date in any year. For example, someone could use a perpetual calendar to find out that July 4, 1776, occurred on a Thursday. The perpetual calendar can also be used to determine days of the week in the future. For example, December 25, 2009, will occur on a Friday.

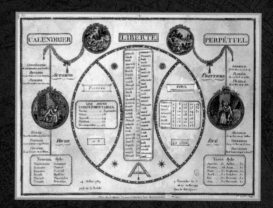

The other main suggestion for a perennial calendar is the World Calendar. It is promoted by the International World Calendar Association. This calendar has four quarters of ninety-one days spread through three months for a total of 364 days. The 365th day would follow December 30 and would be called World Day. In leap years, an extra day would follow June 30 and would be called Leap Year Day. World Day and Leap Year Day would not be numbered nor would they be part of a week or of a month. The World Calendar would make it easier for businesses to make long-range plans and schedules. In 1955, the United Nations General Assembly discussed adopting the World Calendar. At that time, few countries wanted to change to a new calendar, so the matter was dropped. The International World Calendar Association, however, continues to work for calendar reform.

A STANDARD DATING SYSTEM

The way people write dates differs from country to country. For example, an American would write *April 12, 2005*, or *4/12/05*. Someone in England would write *12 April 2005* or *12/4/05*. This date could also be written as *05/4/12* or *05/12/4*. The many ways to write dates can be confusing. The International Organization for Standardization has suggested that everyone in the world write dates starting with the year, then the month, and then the day. April 12, 2005, would be *2005-04-12*.

The Changing Format of Calendars

Since 45 B.C., the way that calendars look has changed greatly. Many of the first Julian calendars were carved in stone tablets and displayed in public areas. Others were painted on the walls of buildings or in homes. Each month a new tablet or wall calendar was made. In the early years of the Christian church, colorful calendars were carved monthly into church doors. Besides days and dates, they had pictures of saints whose feasts were celebrated during the month. They also pictured farming activities for the month.

Gradually, calendars became printed by hand and distributed in book form. These were called books of hours. Again, holy days, saints' days, and farming activities were included. Calendars also formed the framework of books called almanacs. These books included phases of the moon and the hours of daylight for each day. In the 1400s, the printing press was invented. Calendars and almanacs were mass-produced by printing presses and could be found in homes and businesses throughout Europe. In the 1600s, calendars had the days of the week and the dates of the month arranged as a chart. This is like the arrangement of the present-day calendar.

Today, the calendar comes in many forms. Paper calendar books have evolved to daily planner books. Some of them have one or two pages for each day of the year. In addition to the many kinds of paper calendars, people also have

This relief depicting the month of September and the grape harvest was found on a church door in Italy.

BOOK OF HOURS AND THE ALMANAC

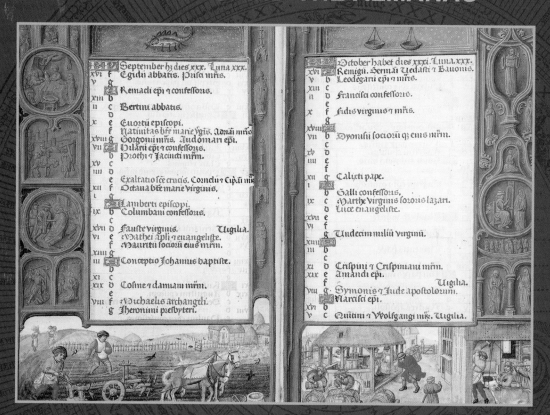

In medieval Europe, books of hours (above) were the main prayer books. Each book contained prayers that were to be said at certain hours of the day and lessons from gospels. A calendar for the year was at the beginning of each book of hours. The Roman numerals in the left hand columns (above) were used to determine the date of Easter and other Feasts. The letters *A* through *G* in the second columns stood for the days of the week. The words written in red marked important feasts and festivals, in this instance for the months of September and October.

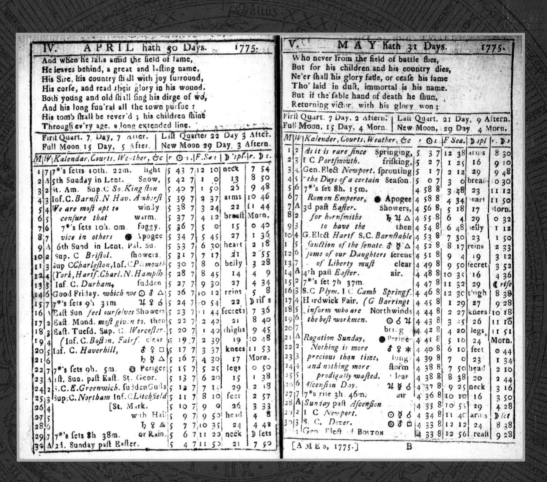

The almanac pages (above) for the months of April and May 1775 provided the reader with much information: the dates for the various phases of the moon, when court hearings would be held in certain towns, weather predictions, and dates for fairs and holidays. When was Easter in 1775?

Daily planners are organized to show one or two days of the year per page.

calendars on their computers. They can bring up their monthly calendar pages and insert appointments, meetings, birthdays, and other events. Appointment calendars are also a feature of cell phones. From stone tablets to cellular phones, the calendar's form has changed throughout history to meet people's need to organize time and lead orderly lives.

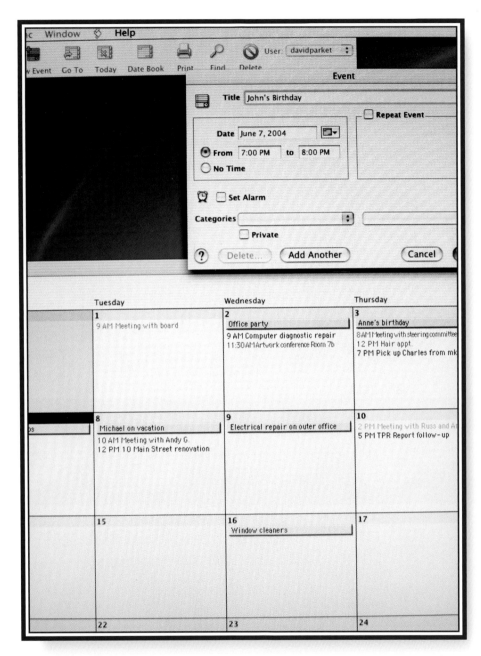

Computer programs offer users calendar pages to insert reminders about meetings and appointments.

Prehistoric people carve a lunar calendar in an animal bone near what is now Dordogne, France.
p. 18

Mesopotamians develop a 360-day calendar.
p. 21

Known as the Year of Confusion, because Julius Caesar added ninety days to the Roman calendar to align it with the solar year.
p. 41

About **28000** B.C.
About **2600** B.C.
About **2100** B.C.
700 B.C.
46 B.C.

Mesopotamians develop the first written calendar.
p. 21

Babylonians have a seven-day week; The Roman year increases to twelve months, with 355 days.
pp. 21, 25

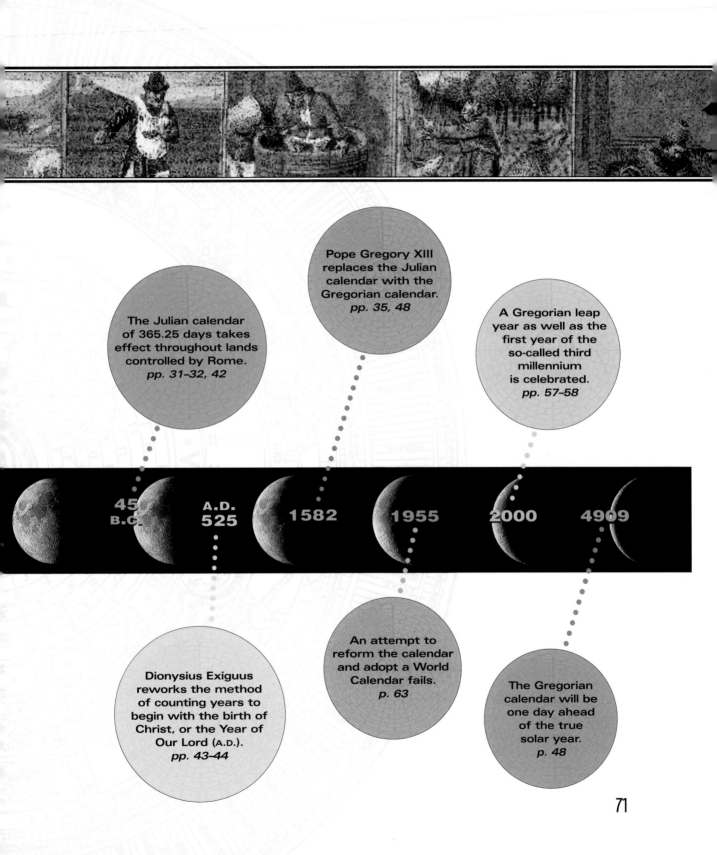

The Julian calendar of 365.25 days takes effect throughout lands controlled by Rome.
pp. 31–32, 42

Pope Gregory XIII replaces the Julian calendar with the Gregorian calendar.
pp. 35, 48

A Gregorian leap year as well as the first year of the so-called third millennium is celebrated.
pp. 57–58

Dionysius Exiguus reworks the method of counting years to begin with the birth of Christ, or the Year of Our Lord (A.D.).
pp. 43–44

An attempt to reform the calendar and adopt a World Calendar fails.
p. 63

The Gregorian calendar will be one day ahead of the true solar year.
p. 48

45 B.C.

A.D. 525

1582

1955

2000

4909

71

GLOSSARY

A.D.: Abbreviation for the Latin term *Anno Domini*, which means "In the Year of the Lord" or the year in which Jesus Christ was born; placed in front of the year number

B.C.: Abbreviation for *Before Christ*, placed after years that occurred before the birth of Jesus Christ

BCE: Abbreviation for *Before the Common Era,* which is often used in place of B.C.

calendar: A way of arranging the days of the year into months and weeks; a table showing the days of the week for every month of the year

CE: Abbreviation for *Common Era*, which is often used in place of A.D.

common year: A year that is not a leap year

day: The period of time it takes the earth to make a complete rotation on its axis

fiscal year: The twelve-month period used by businesses for determining profits and losses

leap year: A year of 366 days; a year that can be evenly divided by four, or in the case of a year ending in two zeroes, one that can be evenly divided by four hundred

lunar calendar: A calendar with a twelve-month year of about 354 days, based on the cycles of the moon

lunisolar calendar: A calendar that bases its year on the phases of the moon but inserts a month every two or three years to become in line with the solar calendar

month: The length of time from one new moon to the next new moon; about 29.5 days

phases of the moon: The varied appearance of the moon during the course of one month

sequential: Following in order

solar calendar: A calendar that bases its year on the length of time it takes the earth to make one revolution around the sun

week: A period of seven days

year: The length of time for the earth to make one revolution around the sun; rounded to 365 days, but actually 365.24219 days

TO FIND OUT MORE

Books

Brimner, Larry. *The Official M&M's Brand Book of the Millennium*. Watertown, Mass.: Charlesbridge Publishing, 1999.

De Bourgoing, Jacqueline. *The Calendar: History, Lore, and Legend*. New York: Harry N. Abrams, Inc., 2001.

Fernández-Armesto, Felipe. *Ideas That Changed the World*. New York: DK Publishing, Inc., 2003.

Maestro, Betsy. *The Story of Clocks and Calendars: Marking a Millennium*. New York: Lothrop, Lee & Shepard Books, 1999.

Skurzynski, Gloria. *On Time: From Seasons to Split Seconds*. Washington, D.C.: National Geographic Society, 2002.

Williams, Brian. *Calendars* (About Time series). North Mankato, Minn.: Smart Apple Media, 2003.

Video

Time and Date. Arc Media, Inc., 1999. CD-ROM with PC and Macintosh versions. Information, games, and quizzes for three different levels about time measurement, the calendar, clocks, and watches.

Web Sites

Calendar Reform

http://www.calendarreform.org

History of the calendar and proposals for calendar reform that would be used worldwide.

Calendars Through the Ages

http://www.webexhibits.org/calendars

Information about the history of many calendars throughout history around the world.

Today's Calendar and Clock Page

http://www.ecben.net/calendar.shtml

This site includes history of the calendar, stories about many of the world's current calendars, a way to convert Gregorian dates to dates on other calendars, holidays throughout the world, and ways to reform the Gregorian calendar; updated daily.

World Wide Leap Year Birthday Club

http://www.leapyearcapital.com

Web site of the Leap Year Capital of the World, the town of Anthony, Texas/New Mexico, with pages about the group's history, past leap-year festivals, and how to join its Leap Year Birthday Club for those born on February 29.

Organizations

Calendar Marketing Association
214 N. Hale St.
Wheaton, IL 60187
630-579-3264

International Organization for Standardization
1, Rue de Varembé, Case Postale 56
CH-1211 Geneva 20, Switzerland

International World Calendar Association
19 Water St.
Brunswick, ME 04011

INDEX

almanacs, 64, 67, *67*

Anno Domini (A.D.), 44

annual calendars, 61

Arabic numerals, 46

archaeology, 18–19

astronomy, 6, *7*, 9, 20, 23–24, 38, 46

Augustus Caesar, 42

Aztec calendar, *5*

Babylon, 21–22

Before the Common Era (BCE), 56

bones, carved, 18, *19*

books of hours, 64, 66, *66*

Buoncompagni, Ugo. *See* Gregory XIII, Pope

Calendar Marketing Association, 56

Calendar of Reason, 59, *60*, 61

calendars
  changing format, 64, 68
  church reform, 32, 34–36, 42–44, 47–50
  definition, 6

industry, 55, *55*

kinds of, 10, *11*, *12*, 12–13, 18–20, 20

selling and marketing, 55

units of time, 8–9

Catholic Church, 32, 34, 42–44, 47

cave painting, 19, *19*

Chinese calendar, 13, 21, 51–52, *52*

Christianity, 43–44

Clavius, Christopher, 34–36, *35*

Common Era (CE), 56

computer calendar, *69*

Constantine, 43

Council of Nicaea, 43

Council of Trent, 32, 34

cultural calendar, 13, 51–52, *52*

day planner, *16*, *68*

days, 8

Diocletian, 44

Dionysius Exiguus, 43–44

dog days, 24

Easter, 43, *45*

economy, 16, 53, 54

Egyptian calendars, 22–24, *23*

farmers/farming, 23

Ford, Henry, 15

French Revolution, 59, 61

Gregorian calendar, 32, 34–36,
    47–50

Gregory XIII, Pope, 32, *33*,
    34–36, *35*

Hebrew calendar, 13, 49, 51–52

ides, 26

Ides of March, 26, 32

illumination from 1400s, *18*

International Fixed Calendar, 61–62

International Organization for
    Standardization, 63

International World
    Calendar Association, 63

inventions, 13–16

Islamic calendar, 10, 49, *49*, 51–52

Italian church door relief, *65*

John I, 43

Julian calendar, 31–32, 38–42, 52

Julius Caesar, 29–32, *30*

kalends, 25

Lascaux caves, 19, *19*

leap years, 12, 32, 57

Lilius, Aloysius and Antonio, 34–35

lunar calendars, 10, *11*, 21

lunar month, 8–9, *9*

lunisolar calendars, 13, 21, 25

mathematics, 38, 42, 46

Mayan calendar, 24, *24*

Mesopotamian calendars, 21, *22*

millennium, 57–58

months, 8–9

moon phases/cycles, 8–9, *9*, 10,
    17–18

mosaic, third century, *40*

New Year's Eve, 58, *58*

nones, 25–26

numbering, 25–26

Omar Khayyam, 28, *28*

Orthodox Church, 47, 52

pauper's calendars, 54, *54*

perennial calendars, 61

perpetual calendar, 62, *62*

Pompey, 30

prehistoric calendars, 18–20, *20*

printing and publishing, 36, 55

red-letter days, 27

reform commission, 34, 35, 35, 47–50

religious calendars, 51–52

Roman calendars, 25–27, 26, 31, 37

sequential calendars, 9

Sirius, 23, 23, 24

solar calendars, 12, 12, 22–24

solar year, 9

solstice, 20

Sosigenes, 30, 31, 39

stonehenge, 20, 20

time

    ancient forms of keeping, 5–6

    calendar units, 8

    early reasons for keeping, 17–18, 20

    sequential, 6, *8*

timeline, 70–71

trade, 16, 46

travel, 16

tropical year, 9

weeks, 10

Whitney, Eli, 15

World Calendar, 63

World Wide Leap Year Birthday Club, 57

written calendars, 21

Year of Confusion, 41

ABOUT THE AUTHOR

Patricia K. Kummer writes and edits nonfiction books for children and young adults from her home office in Lisle, Illinois. She earned a bachelor of arts degree in history from the College of St. Catherine in St. Paul, Minnesota, and a master of arts degree in history from Marquette University in Milwaukee, Wisconsin. Before starting her career in publishing, she taught social studies at the junior high/ middle school level. Since then, she has written books about American, African, Asian, and European history. She also has written six books (*Côte d'Ivoire, Ukraine, Tibet, Singapore, Cameroon, and Korea*) in the Children's Press series Enchantment of the World and *Currency* in the Franklin Watts series Inventions That Shaped the World.

Ms. Kummer hopes that this book will help young people better understand how the calendar developed and the important role that it plays in daily life.